Look & Wonder

Gods & Goddesses

Created and designed by

David Salariya

Written by

Jacqueline Morley

MACDONALD YOUNG BOOKS

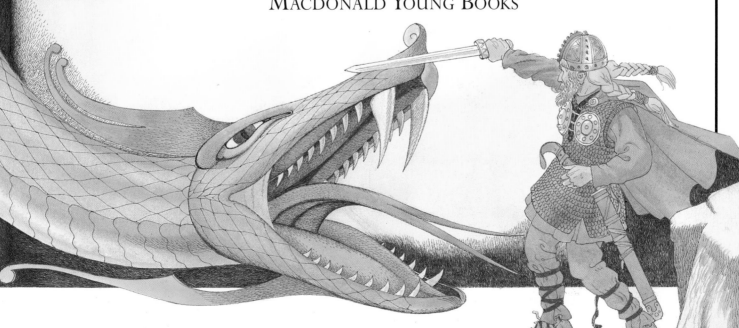

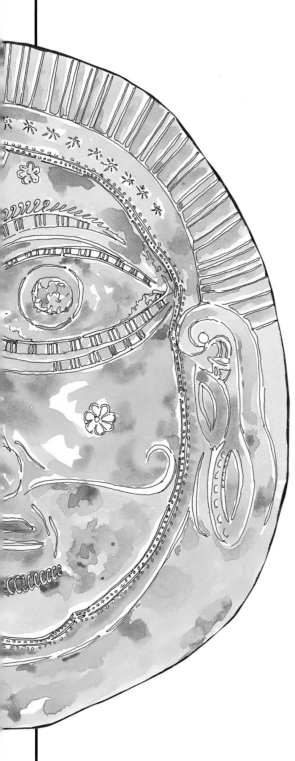

Contents

World of the gods

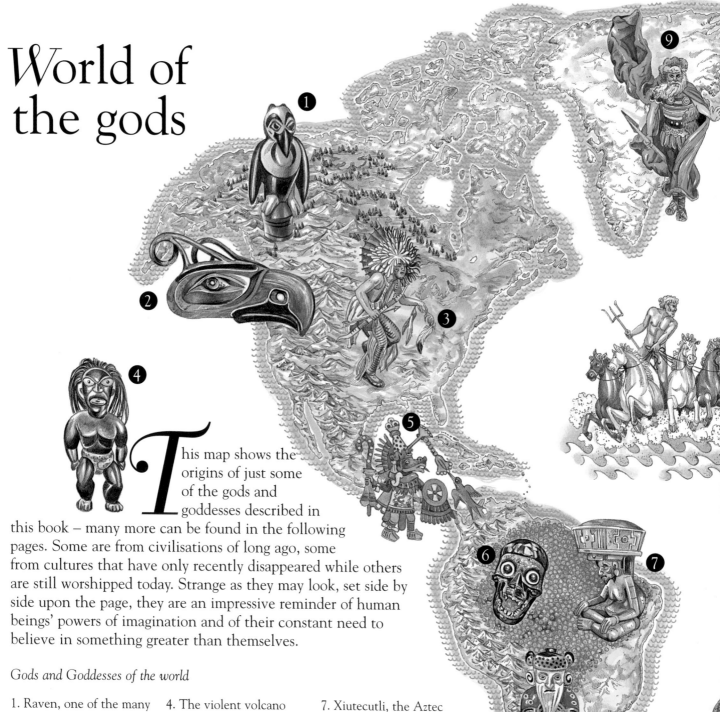

This map shows the origins of just some of the gods and goddesses described in this book – many more can be found in the following pages. Some are from civilisations of long ago, some from cultures that have only recently disappeared while others are still worshipped today. Strange as they may look, set side by side upon the page, they are an impressive reminder of human beings' powers of imagination and of their constant need to believe in something greater than themselves.

Gods and Goddesses of the world

1. Raven, one of the many animal trickster gods of north America.
2. A North American thunderbird mask. Thunder, lightning, and other violent natural events were thought to be the work of the gods.
3. A Plains Indian medicine man. Shaman, medicine man and witch doctor are all names for a person believed to have special powers for contacting the spirit world.

4. The violent volcano goddess Pele lives in a crater on the Pacific island of Hawaii.
5. Quetzalcoatl, the plumed serpent, one of the gods worshipped by the Aztecs of Central America before the Spaniards arrived.
6. Tezcatlipoca, the Aztec god of dark powers, misfortune, war and death. He was the enemy of Quetzalcoatl, whom he defeated.

7. Xiutecutli, the Aztec fire god.
8. Viracocha, supreme god of the Incas of Peru.
9. Odin, ruler of the Norse gods who were worshipped in Scandinavia and northern Europe. Vikings took tales of the Norse gods to Iceland.
10. Thor, Odin's fiery son.
11. Devil mask from Slovenia.
12. Cernunnos, a god of the ancient Celtic peoples of Europe.

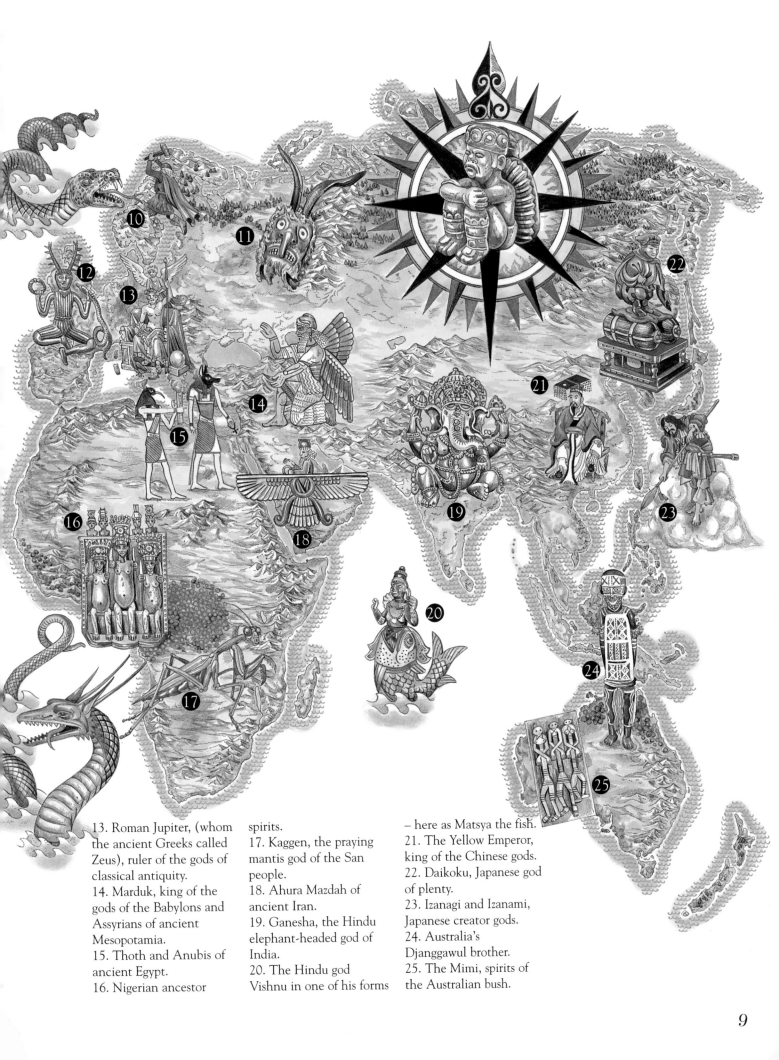

13. Roman Jupiter, (whom the ancient Greeks called Zeus), ruler of the gods of classical antiquity.

14. Marduk, king of the gods of the Babylons and Assyrians of ancient Mesopotamia.

15. Thoth and Anubis of ancient Egypt.

16. Nigerian ancestor spirits.

17. Kaggen, the praying mantis god of the San people.

18. Ahura Mazdah of ancient Iran.

19. Ganesha, the Hindu elephant-headed god of India.

20. The Hindu god Vishnu in one of his forms – here as Matsya the fish.

21. The Yellow Emperor, king of the Chinese gods.

22. Daikoku, Japanese god of plenty.

23. Izanagi and Izanami, Japanese creator gods.

24. Australia's Djanggawul brother.

25. The Mimi, spirits of the Australian bush.

Introduction

This is a collection of gods and goddesses from around the world – the most beautiful, the most frightening, the oddest, the kindliest and the most evil beings that humanity has been able to imagine. The tales of their deeds have been told and retold for generations and offer explanations for the mysterious and often terrifying world people found themselves living in.

Such stories are often called myths. They tell of gods and goddesses who interfere with daily life, are jealous, unreasonable or simply evil. Such beings seem remote and perhaps unbelievable in today's high-tech world. However, the basic human need to make sense of life still exists. Belief in gods and goddesses may help find the answers to such questions as 'how did the world begin?', 'why are so many things wrong with it?', 'how could it be made better?' and 'what happens when we die?'. The modern world's religions and scientific discoveries may still leave these questions unanswered.

No wonder then, that early peoples, with no ideas but their own to guide them, imagined the world to be full of invisible powers. All over the world these powers have been given different names and forms by different cultures and have been worshipped, revered or feared as gods and goddesses.

The myths that surround the gods and goddesses described here express ideas that their worshippers firmly believed to be true. Today they may appear to be simply good stories, but for their creators they signified the greatest and most important things – the beginning and end, creation and destruction, life and death.

In the beginning

Almost all mythologies include a story of a great god or goddess who created the world. But what existed in the beginning, before the gods? Curiously enough, many traditions agree that the first of all things must have been an endless sea. The ancient Egyptians called this watery vastness Nun and believed that the god Ra, who represented light, arose from Nun and created the world. The Greeks named it Chaos, from which came the goddess Gaia, who was the earth, the mother of everything. The Babylonians believed the water had both male and female forms called Apsu and Tiamat. When the two forms of water mixed, the gods were born.

Another widely held belief was that all things came from an egg. According to a Chinese tale, the egg burst open because it could no longer hold the giant P'an-ku, who had been growing inside it for 18,000 years. He thrust its halves apart to form the earth and sky. When he died, his limbs became the mountains, his left eye the sun, his right eye the moon, his hair the trees and plants and his tears the seas. Human beings are said to be descended from his fleas.

The Aztec serpent-god Quetzalcoatl (above) coiled himself around an alligator-monster, Cipactli, who swam in the first waters, and squeezed her in two to make the earth and sky.

The Assyrian god Marduk (right), became king of the gods by defeating Tiamat, which was the cruel sea in dragon form. Marduk thrust a whirlwind down Tiamat's throat, sliced her in two and made the earth and sky from the pieces.

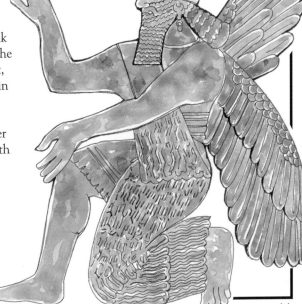

Creator gods

After the world was made, where did life come from? Many myths say it was born from the marriage of the earth and sky. The ancient Greeks told how Gaia took Uranus, the sky, as her husband and then poured forth multitudes of creatures – land and sea beasts and the first race of gods, the Titans.

Human beings often appear quite late in such stories. The Greeks believed that the Titan Prometheus modelled them from clay. The Mesopotamian god Marduk made humans as a servant race, to save the gods the trouble of looking after the world.

Often some mishap in their creation accounts for inequalities between humans. The Chinese 'August Personage of Jade' made people from earth and put them out to dry. When he saw it was raining he rushed to bring them in but some had gone soft. These became the sick and feeble.

Some gods were far less admirable. There is a widespread belief in a trickster god, often up to no good, who sometimes takes the form of a creator. Maui of the South Pacific is one; he made the Pacific islands by pulling them up from the sea. To make daytime longer he lassoed the sun and beat it so hard that now it can only creep across the sky. As the sky was inconveniently low he pushed it up with a poker; the dark marks the poker left are storm clouds.

This Maori version of Maui shows him creating North Island, New Zealand by hauling it up from the ocean bed. The island is represented by a fish.

The Ancient Egyptian god Ra created the world by uttering the names of things.

Ra named Shu, the wind and Tefnut, the rain. He named Geb, and the earth appeared. He named Nut, and the sky goddess arched over the earth.

The Polynesians believe their god Tangaroa made the world. They say that at first there was only sea. Then Tangaroa came out of a mussel shell and made the land and living things. He was lord of the sea creatures and often quarrelled with his brother, the forest god Tane. Tane gave men wooden canoes and taught them to fish. In revenge, Tangaroa overturned the boats and drowned the fishermen. This carving (left) shows him covered with the land and sea creatures he created. It is a hollow carving and there are more creatures inside.

Japanese legend tells how Izanagi and his sister Izanami, children of the First Being, stood on the bridge of heaven and stirred the waters of the universe with a jewelled spear. Drops of water falling from the spear formed a tiny islet where the two settled. They became the parents of many gods and of the Japanese islands.

In Hindu mythology the universe is destroyed and remade in an endless cycle over vast periods of time. Brahma is its creator, and each of his days and nights is equal to 8,640,000,000 of our years. The world lasts a century of such days, dies and is reborn. Brahma renews the universe from a golden egg that floats on the first endless waters. This painting (right) shows him tending a sacred fire while the holy River Ganges flows beneath him. Brahma has four heads – he grew the extra ones in order to gaze on his beautiful wife Sarasvati wherever she was.

The earth, sea and sky

It is taken for granted that the sun will rise tomorrow, but for early civilisations, nothing in nature happened without a reason or a driving force. For the sun to rise, a sun god must have steered it across the sky and disappeared in the west. If he decided not to return, the dark would last for ever. A sea god kept the waves within its bounds and a rain god sent the water on which life depended.

However, such mighty beings acted mostly to please themselves. Sometimes they neglected their duties, with disastrous consequences. When Helios, the Greek sun god, let his inexperienced son drive the sun's chariot it ran out of control and set the earth on fire.

It was equally dangerous for humans to neglect the gods. If they did not receive proper worship the gods were quick to take offence. The Inuit people of the North American Arctic believed it was vital to please Igaluk the moon spirit, the hunter of the sky. They had to return to him, by magical means, the souls of all creatures killed for food or fur. Only then would he send them more.

The seated figure in this Babylonian relief (above) is the moon god, Sin. He is old and wise, the father of the sun and the measurer of time. Since he lights the night he is the enemy of those who use it to hide evil deeds.

The searing heat of India's dry season accounts for the legend of Surya, the Hindu sun god. His wife feared she would be shrivelled by his rays and asked the craftsman god Visvakarma to shave the ends off them. He made the burning tips into weapons for the gods.

Rain was so important to the Aztecs that they sacrificed children to their rain god, Tlaloc. This scene (above) from a pyramid at Teotihucan, Mexico, shows Tlaloc showering water to make corn grow.

In the beginning, say the Amazonian people, it was always day. The great king god Cobra kept night hidden in the bed of the river. When people complained that they could not sleep he gave them a coconut, telling them not to open it until they got home. They disobeyed and night shot out, plunging them into blackness.

Poseidon rode the seas in a chariot drawn by creatures that were half horse, half sea-serpent.

Poseidon, lord of the ocean (left), was the hot-tempered sea god of the ancient Greeks. With a flourish of his trident he created storms and floods, made rivers dry up or springs burst from the ground.

15

Imir the frost giant

The Norse creation story

Before the world was made, two realms existed, one of fire and the other of freezing fog and ice. Between them was a vast space called the Yawning Gap. There came a time when a flicker of fire crossed the Yawning Gap and met a blast of cold from the land of ice. Then, like steam forming on a mirror, water appeared and, drip, drip, drip, it fell into the Yawning Gap. This water gave life to the first being: a giant whose name was Imir.

Imir was an evil giant, made of frost. As he slept in his bed of icy sludge, sons and daughters sprang out of his arms and legs, until there was a whole tribe of savage frost giants in the Yawning Gap. They fed on streams of milk from a giant cow which had grown out of the melting ice.

The cow grazed on the ice as if it were grass and as she licked she uncovered the hair, and then the head, of a man. She licked and licked all day until his arms and chest appeared and the next day she licked until the whole man was born from the ice. He was big and strong and his name was Buri. Buri had a son called Bor who married the daughter of a frost giant and their three children became the great gods Odin, Vili and Ve.

Odin and his brothers waged war on the hateful frost giants and killed Imir. A river of blood flowed from his wounds. The gods formed earth from Imir's flesh and mountains from his bones. His skull became the dome of the sky and his blood the seas. With sparks from the realm of fire the brothers created the sun, the moon and the stars and set them in the sky.

Then Odin found two fallen trees by the seashore, an ash and an elm. He took a branch from each and made them into living creatures, a man called Ask (ash) and a woman called Embla (elm), and these were the ancestors of all people.

Death and destruction

The sense that evil exists in the world is as basic to human nature as a small child's fear of the dark. How did the evil get here? Most mythologies accept evil as a fact of life and describe gods who represent it. Evil is frequently misshapen and disordered and it is commonly believed that things are put in order by creator gods, who represent good. In the Norse mythology of northern Europe the evil god was Loki, a murderer and father of monsters. In North America it was the trickster Coyote. The Californian Maidu people say he brought death and all manner of evil into the world while the Apache blamed him for the arrival of the Europeans.

The face of a nightmare – Medusa the Gorgon. There were three sister Gorgons, deadly winged monsters with snakes for hair, whose glance turned people to stone. Medusa was the mother of Pegasus, a winged horse, shown tucked under her arm.

A host of monsters, demons and spirits seem to have plagued humanity. The ancient Greeks had Gorgons, many-headed Hydras and Hecate of the dark, who lingered where roads crossed. The Celts believed in The Morrigan, red-haired goddess of conflict, who appeared as a raven when the dying littered a battlefield. In central African forests there were the elokos – dwarf-demons who ate human flesh and were masters of witchcraft. The Aztecs took a particularly fearful view of existence. To them the universe was poised on the brink of destruction; only constant sacrifices to the gods preserved it. The most effective sacrifice was believed to be human life. The fact that all Aztec gods required such sacrifices reveals less about Aztec cruelty than about Aztec fears.

This mask, shaped over a human skull and set with turquoise, represents Tezcatlipoca, or 'smoking mirror', the Aztec god of war and vengeance. He was the god of sorcerers too, for in his magic mirror he saw all things and read all thoughts.

Reciting spells, wearing amulets or performing ritual dances were ways of robbing evil gods of their power to harm. This North American Iroquois mask (right) of painted wood and human hair was worn in such ceremonies.

In the underworld

The idea of a land where the dead dwell was common. It was often an underground place of judgment. Jigoku, the Japanese hell, had eight regions of fire and eight of ice, all the domain of a stern judge, Emmahoo. There, the past sins of the dead were reflected back to them by a huge mirror. The ancient Greek underworld was the realm of the god Hades. Most of the dead led a twilight existence there as shadows of their living selves. Luckier souls went to the happy Elysian fields but the wicked entered the bronze gates of Tartarus. Greeks were buried with a coin in their mouths to pay Charon, the boatman who ferried the dead across the River Styx to Hade's kingdom.

The ancient Egyptians believed the land of souls was just like Egypt, but without poverty or problems. Its king was Osiris, a god who had died and come to life again. However, his realm had many regions, full of terrors which Ra, the sun god, fought with nightly as he steered the sun's boat through the underworld to reach dawn.

Above, a pottery figure of Mictlantecuhli, the Aztec lord of Mictlan, an underground world of shadows. On their way there the dead were reduced to skeletons by a wind of knives.

Yen-Lo Wang, the Chinese god of death, was the chief of ten judges who decided the fate of the dead. Sentences were matched to crimes (liars had to swallow molten gold) and devils chased the damned to their fate.

One way of coping with fear of the powers of darkness was to make fun of them. This image of a Slovenian carnival mask portrays the Christian devil as both horrible and comic.

A Zapotec clay head, (right) sad on one side, skull-like on the other, represents life and death. The gods of the Zapotecs, like those of the Aztecs who conquered them, demanded human sacrifices.

Viking evildoers went to a place of bitter cold and screaming winds when they died – the realm of hideous Queen Hel. Its entrance was guarded by the blood-spattered hound Garmr who was kept chained to prevent him ravaging the upper world.

Anubis, the Egyptian jackal-headed burial god, led a soul to judgment (above). The dead man's heart was put in the scales to see if his bad deeds outweighed the Feather of Truth.

Thoth, god of writing, noted the results (below). Heavy hearts were eaten by the monster waiting by the scales, but good souls were presented to Osiris who welcomed them.

Gods and men destroyed

There are many stories of the terrible destruction that the gods may cause. Usually human beings are the victims, because of their wickedness. The Egyptian god Ra sent Semkhet, a raging lion goddess, to destroy mankind. Her thirst for blood was so terrible that even Ra was sorry. He managed to stop her by tricking her into drinking red-stained beer instead. A tradition found all over the world tells of a dreadful flood. The story of Noah's ark is one version of it, while the Mayans believed that the moon-goddess Ixchel drowned the world by emptying the vessel of doom. In Chinese legend the green-faced thunder god caused the flood, and in Hindu beliefs the god Vishnu came to earth as a fish in order to save one good man from the waters.

Stranger than any of these tales is the Norse prophecy of the destruction of the gods themselves, at Ragnarok, the day of doom. No one was sure when this dreaded day would come but a bitter winter, three years long, would herald it. On that day, it was said, the Earth's crust will split and hideous powers will break the chains with which the gods have bound them. The evil god Loki will come with an army of the dead, in a ship made of dead men's nails. The frost giants and the fire giants will join him, together with Loki's fearsome sons: the World Serpent that encircles the seas and Fenrir, the giant with gaping jaws. Against these monsters the gods will fight the Last Battle and be overcome. Thor will be killed by the poisonous breath of the World Serpent and Odin will ride into the jaws of Fenrir, which will close upon him. Then earth and heaven will disappear in smoke and darkness.

The legend of Unkulunkulu

Unkulunkulu the Great One, ancestor of the Zulu people of Africa, made the first men and women from reeds. He put the sun and moon in the sky and filled the earth with wild creatures. Then he made cattle, sheep and goats for his people and gave them water to drink and fire to cook with. He was pleased with what he had done. He called the chameleon to him and said "Take a message to the people of the world. Tell them, people shall not die."

The chameleon was proud to be given such an important task. It set off at once, at a very slow, stately pace, for that is a chameleon's way. It repeated the message as it crept along, "People shall not die. People shall not die", to make sure it got it right.

Meanwhile, Unkulunkulu was having second thoughts. He called the lizard and said, "Take this message to the people of the world. Tell them 'All things must die'. All men, all women, all cattle, sheep and goats, all must die".

The lizard darted off. While the chameleon was still cautiously putting down one foot in front of the other and pausing to eat a leaf or two here and there, the lizard had reached the people. It summoned all of them and made its announcement "Everything must perish. All things one day must die."

Some time later, the chameleon's head emerged from the bushes. "I have a message," it said solemnly. But when the people heard the message they cried, "Too late! We have already received the word of Unkulunkulu. The message of the Great One cannot be taken back: "All things must die."

A legacy of gods and goddesses

The gods are by no means things of the past. The ancient gods of India, for example, are still worshipped by Hindus today. Although the gods of the western mythologies may have lost their religious meanings, particular gods and goddesses still have a place in our imagination.

Aphrodite (her ancient Greek name), the irresistible love goddess of the classical world, has never ceased to be celebrated in poems, music, paintings and statues. She was born, fully-grown, from the foam of the sea. As she came ashore flowers sprang up wherever she put her feet. Her Roman name was Venus. The idea that physical beauty is valuable for its own sake is a legacy of Venus. This concept continues in many of today's cultures and values. The beauty queens of the modern world are a distant echo of her and her son Cupid is still known by his appearance on Valentine cards.

Serenely beautiful and mysterious, this head of Aphrodite (below) from about 500 BC expresses the awe-inspiring aspects of the goddess who represented love in all its forms.

In this painting on a Greek cup from about 470 BC, a much daintier Aphrodite travels through the air on a goose, seated elegantly side-saddle. This is the love goddess as an enchantress and stealer of hearts.

Masters of the world

This symbol (above) represents Ahura Mazda, the ancient Iranian lord of the world. He was pure goodness and fought continually with Ahriman, the power of evil. Ahura Mazda was symbolized by fire, a purifying element.

The god who was believed to rule the world was not necessarily its creator. Often the ruler was a mighty warrior who stepped in and defeated evil forces or older gods after another being had carried out creation.

The Mesopotamian gods had to accept Marduk as king because they had all been too cowardly to fight Tiamat. Zeus became lord of the ancient Greek world by getting rid of the Titans, the children of Gaia from whom he was descended. The Norse god Odin defeated the frost giants and then dealt with the terrible offspring of Loki: Fenrir the wolf and Jormungander the serpent. Odin kept Fenrir in chains and flung the serpent into the sea, where it continues to circle the world with its tail in its mouth.

The ancient Chinese god Huangdi ruled as Yellow Emperor (above). Finally, a dragon carried him to heaven, together with his ministers and wives – 70 in all.

The supreme god of the ancient Greeks was Zeus, known to the Romans as Jupiter. In this Roman wall painting (left) Victory crowns him with bay leaves. In his right hand Zeus holds his favourite weapon, a thunderbolt, and at his feet are an eagle and a globe – symbols of his greatness.

In traditional African beliefs everything in nature has a spirit, including the souls of the dead, who continue to be a ruling presence in the world. These 'ancestor spirits' give guidance and protection to relatives who honour them. This altar screen from Nigeria shows ancestor spirits bearing knives and tusks – symbols of power.

Odin, awesome king of the Norse gods, was the lord of battle, magic and poetry. He was very wise but his wisdom cost him an eye. This was the price he paid the giant Mimir for a drink from the well of knowledge. His two ravens, Huginn (thought) and Munnin (memory) kept him informed of all that went on in the world.

War gods are the most important gods in many mythologies. This terrifying wooden image is of the Hawaiian war god Ku. He helped the creator god Kane to make human beings, so he was also revered as the ancestor god of the people of Hawaii.

Vishnu, the most widely honoured Hindu god (pictured below), is known as the Preserver, for he has come to earth many times in different forms to save mankind from evil. During the millions of years between the end of one world and the creation of the next, Vishnu sleeps on a vast ocean, resting under the protection of many-headed Vasuki, king of the Nagas (serpent gods).

Animal gods

Kaggen, chief god of the San people of southern Africa, appears on earth in the shape of a praying mantis. He created the world and made the moon out of an old shoe.

Native Americans of the north Pacific coast tell many stories of Raven, their trickster god (below). Although he is capable of good – he brought light from heaven for earth – he is mischievous and greedy. Once he swallowed the sun and had to be tickled to make him spit it out.

Peoples who live close to nature, as the distant ancestors of all civilisations once did, commonly believed that all natural things – wind, rocks, trees and every living creature – possess a spirit. Animal spirits were especially important for hunting tribes who depended on animals in order to survive. The Ainu of Japan called bears 'That Divine One Reigning in the Mountains'.

Hunters performed rituals to acquire the strength of these animal spirits and ensure success in hunting. Prehistoric drawings of men crowned with antlers, found in countries as far apart as France and China, Canada and Australia, show the ancient origin of these rites. Such images help to show how these people felt at one with animals and gave animal gods human characteristics.

In many African and North American myths, animals have magic powers. In Zaire, the hero Mokele was accompanied by the tortoise Nkulu and the kite Nkombe when he went to get the sun for his people. This was because they only had the moon to see by. Nkulu, the tortoise, was a sorcerer. By magic he discovered the sun where no eye could see it, hidden in a cave by the old chief Mokulaka. The tortoise lifted the sun out of its hiding place and the kite gripped the tortoise in its talons and soared high into the air with both of them. That is how the sun rose for the first time.

A native American thunderbird mask was worn to impersonate one of these powerful birds in a ritual. Thunderbirds were believed to be the storm-makers. Their eyes flashed lightning and their wing-beats were thunderclaps.

Ganesha, the Hindu god of good fortune (below), has the head of an elephant. Legend says that this was the first thing that came to hand when his father, Shiva, unintentionally cut off his son's head and needed a replacement.

Cernunnos, the stag-horned Lord of the Animals, was one of the most powerful Celtic gods (left). He was widely worshipped in Britain and France in pre-Christian times.

Each ancient Egyptian god had some creature sacred to it. Often the gods were shown in human form but with a creature's head. They were also represented by the creature itself. In this statue the cow that is guarding a pharaoh is the protective goddess Hathor.

A sun goddess

According to Japanese legend the greatest deity of all was Amaterasu, the beautiful goddess of the sun. She ruled the heavens justly and took her duty to light and warm the earth seriously. But her brother the storm god was bad-tempered and destructive and gave his sister nothing but trouble. He uprooted trees, blew buildings over and made the whole earth shake. Worse still, he wrecked his sister's work, destroying her fields and dumping filth in her temples. Once he tore a hole in the roof of the building in which she and her attendants sat weaving clothes for the gods. He then dropped the horrible skinned body of a horse on them. At this, Amaterasu could stand no more. She hid in the cave of the heavens, blocked the entrance with a boulder and plunged the world into darkness.

Amaterasu would not come out of the cave and many evil spirits were taking advantage and doing mischief in the dark, so the good gods decided they must lure Amaterasu out. Eight million of them met outside the cave, bringing with them an odd assortment of items – a cockerel (rooster), a mirror, a string of jewels and a wooden tub. First they lit bonfires to make a lot of light and hung the mirror and the jewels on a tree so that they glittered in the flames. Then they made the cock crow as if dawn were coming. Amaterasu, inside her cave, was puzzled. Next she heard music and the sound of laughter, for a young goddess called Uzume was doing a comical dance on the upturned tub. Amaterasu pushed the stone aside a fraction and saw light flashing from the jewels.

"What's going on?" she called.

"We're welcoming the new sun," Uzume called back. "She shines much brighter than you did!"

Amaterasu felt she had to take a proper look. She made the gap a little wider, saw herself reflected in the mirror and pushed the stone right back, to dazzle what she believed to be her rival. Immediately, one of the gods dragged her from the cave and another hung a magic rope of straw across the entrance to stop her going back. All the eight million gods burst out laughing. Amaterasu laughed too when she saw her mistake and since that time the sun has never failed to shine when it should.

The fierce and the friendly

A god or goddess could not be judged by appearance. Some of the most ferocious-looking were kind and some of the beautiful were truly evil. It did not worry the ancient Egyptians that Tavaret, the goddess who cared for women in childbirth, looked like a hideous hippopotamus. Whatever the gods' appearance (evil Loki of Norse legend was good looking), it was usually clear from their actions whether they were dangerous or not.

However, the Hindu mother-goddess Devi is both mild and ruthless, kind and cruel. She has many personalities, each with a different name, for she represents nature in all its aspects – creating, sustaining and destroying. As Devi, she is the loving mother of humanity. When evil, she becomes the warrior goddess Durga who slays demons. In her most terrible form she is Kali the Destroyer, with a red lolling tongue, a necklace of skulls and a girdle of severed arms. How can one goddess be all these things? It is because she represents the multitude of characteristics present in nature and reflected in many aspects of life.

This north Australian figure is of a quite friendly god. He and his two sisters are known as the Djanggawul. They came from beyond the sea and taught people to dig waterholes and grow crops.

Durga looks alarming, with ten arms poised to kill (right), but she defends mankind. In this form Devi slaughtered the seemingly indestructible buffalo-demon Mahisha and so became the supreme Hindu deity.

Angry gods

Everywhere, people have interpreted the violence of nature – volcanoes, earthquakes, storms and floods – as signs that the gods were angry. In places where such events were common, it was natural to suppose that the god responsible was both very powerful and bad-tempered. Especially temperamental were the goddess Pele in volcanic Hawaii, and Hurakan, the lord of the whirlwinds, in the hurricane-ridden West Indies. The earthquake goddess, Masaya, lived below ground in Nicaragua so after an earthquake human victims were thrown into her craters to appease her.

Lightning was the weapon of the kings of the gods. The ancient Greek god Zeus wielded it and in India it belonged to Indra, the ruler of the sky. The Chinese believed lightning struck those who were guilty of undetected crimes. The peoples of Zambia and Angola, where hurricanes and dust storms are frequent, say that these are a sign that the sky god Leza has had one of his rages. Long ago, Leza lived on earth under a huge tree and villagers had to bring him sheep and goats to eat. One day a gigantic dust cloud covered the village. It was Leza. He told the assembled villagers that they would never see him again but he would be watching them from the sky. The sight of a shooting star shows that Leza is keeping an eye on them.

When Aborigine tribesmen in Australia are out in the bush they shout occasionally to make sure they do not take the Mimi (left) by surprise. These ghostly beings, as long and thin as the rock crevices from which they appear, are harmless if left alone but if disturbed they can cause sickness or death.

Set (left), god of the hostile desert, sent the drought and sand-laden winds the ancient Egyptians dreaded. Ra put Set's savagery to good use by making him defend the sun's boat. Apophis, the serpent of evil, attempted to overcome the sun each night.

Left, the terrifying figure of Pele, the Hawaiian volcano goddess. Hawaiians say she came from the island of Tahiti, as their ancestors did. She had to leave it because her family would not put up with her bad temper. Pele arrived amid flashes of lightning and made her home in the crater of Mount Kilauea. When she gets angry she spouts boiling lava.

Tonatiuh, the Aztec sun god, is depicted with an earthquake on his back. The Aztecs believed that this is the world of the fifth sun. Four previous worlds have ended in disaster. This one will end in an earthquake.

Ancient Greek Pan, the herdsmen's goat-like god, embodied the dangerous, unpredictable nature of the wild. The word 'panic' comes from his name. Above he is shown teaching a shepherd boy to play the pan-pipes.

The providers

Without the will of the gods, nothing was possible, so it followed that every provision in life was a gift from them. Most regions have or had their own variety of myths involving a crop bringer. The ancient Greeks honoured Demeter, the corn goddess, and Dionysus, god of the vine, who taught people how to make wine from grapes. The Mayans of central America honoured Yum Kaax the maize god. In Japan every village had a shrine to the rice god Inari, a kind, bearded old man. Inari was also a god of prosperity, for good fortune, health and happiness were all gifts from the gods.

The most precious gift of all was fire. It seems that it was so precious, gods tried to keep it to themselves – the tale that it was stolen from them appears in many mythologies. According to the ancient Greeks, Prometheus the Titan brought fire down from Mount Olympus, hidden in a hollow fennel stalk. The Creek Indians of Alabama say that Rabbit, their trickster god, stole it. He crossed the Great Water to the land of the Fire People and joined their dance. The Fire People bowed low to the Sacred Fire as they danced around it, but not as low as Rabbit who bowed until his cap caught fire. Then he ran and the Fire People followed, but they would not cross the water. Rabbit swam across with his head ablaze and so brought fire into the world.

Dionysus the Greek wine god was a wild reveller. He travelled in a chariot drawn by panthers and sometimes drove his worshippers to madness. The picture (above) is based on a scene found on a vase from about 480 BC.

A luxuriantly decorated Roman sarcophagus (similar to that pictured left) of the 3rd century AD depicts Bacchus (the Roman equivalent of Dionysus). He is seated on his panther and flanked by figures representing the four seasons. The god and his attendants are dignified and serene, quite unlike their Greek counterparts. In late classical times myths were interpreted symbolically. Here the ecstasy of the wine god symbolised the joy of the soul's union with the gods after death.

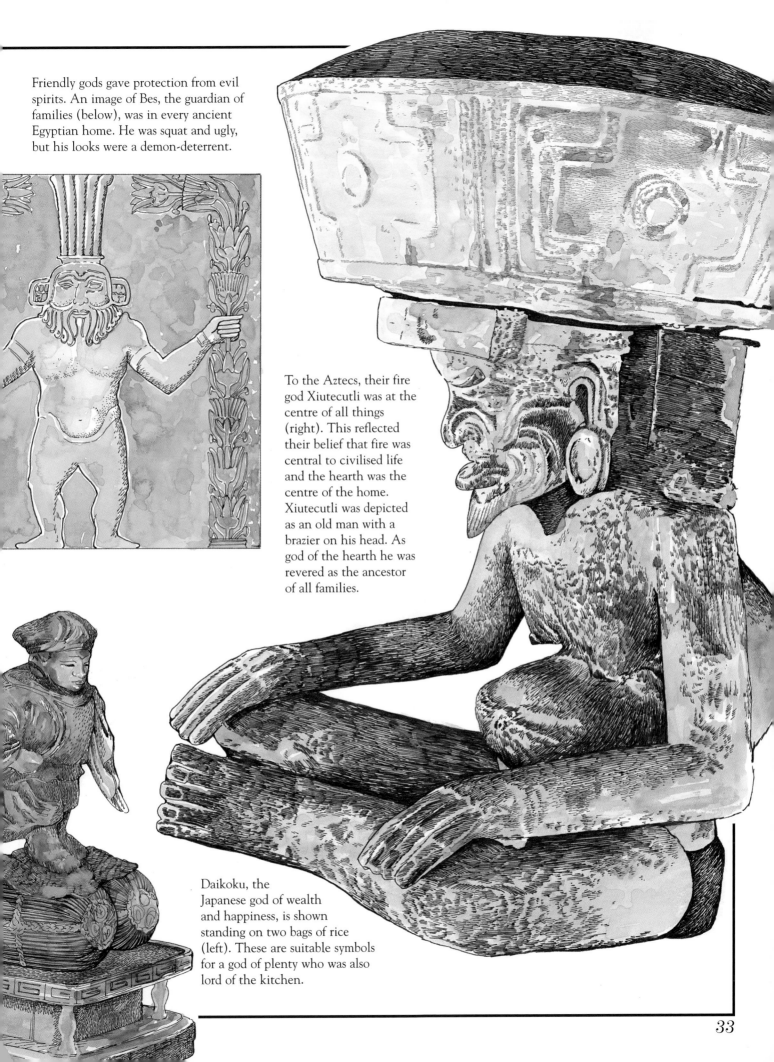

Friendly gods gave protection from evil spirits. An image of Bes, the guardian of families (below), was in every ancient Egyptian home. He was squat and ugly, but his looks were a demon-deterrent.

To the Aztecs, their fire god Xiutecutli was at the centre of all things (right). This reflected their belief that fire was central to civilised life and the hearth was the centre of the home. Xiutecutli was depicted as an old man with a brazier on his head. As god of the hearth he was revered as the ancestor of all families.

Daikoku, the Japanese god of wealth and happiness, is shown standing on two bags of rice (left). These are suitable symbols for a god of plenty who was also lord of the kitchen.

A story of the seasons

An ancient Greek myth

In the beginning there was no winter. Flowers bloomed and crops ripened the whole year round. Demeter, the harvest goddess, kept the world in this happy state. She was the power that made all green things grow.

Demeter had a daughter called Persephone who was as good and kind as she was beautiful. Hades, king of the underworld, wanted her to be his queen. He went to his brother Zeus and demanded that he arrange the match. Zeus knew that Demeter would never let her daughter be taken to the gloomy underworld so he invented excuses to put the matter off. Hades returned to the underworld in a fury and made his own plans.

Persephone was picking flowers one day in the meadows when suddenly the ground beside her cracked and parted and Hades in his black chariot came thundering out. He snatched Persephone up and galloped away with her into the earth.

When Demeter discovered her daughter had vanished she was overcome with grief. She wandered all over the earth, looking in vain for her. At last, worn out, she sank down by the bank of a stream.

"My waters rise in the heart of the earth," the stream whispered to her. "As I flowed past Hades' palace I saw Persephone there, pale and sad, seated on a throne beside him."

Demeter vowed that until Hades restored her daughter to her she would let nothing grow. Crops withered, seeds rotted in the ground and people began to starve. Soon even the gods grew worried. Zeus realised that he must make his brother see sense and give Persephone back.

Hades seemed ready to agree, provided that Persephone had not eaten anything while she was in the underworld. He knew he had coaxed her into eating seven pomegranate seeds. Persephone confessed this was true. She had eaten the food of the dead, which meant she belonged to the underworld forever.

Even Zeus could not alter this law, but he made Hades accept a compromise. Half of each year Persephone should spend underground with him and the other half with her mother. It is Demeter's grief at parting with her daughter that makes trees shed their leaves and plants die back into the ground during autumn and winter. But when Persephone returns to her once more, green shoots appear and it is spring again.

Meeting the gods

Many myths tell of mortals meeting the gods, at times without recognising them. When the Greek hero Jason carried a mournful old woman across a swollen river, she transformed herself on the far bank into Hera, wife of the king of the gods, and promised to reward him. Irish Cuchulainn was less courteous. When he met a fearsome woman with red eyebrows driving a chariot with a one-eyed, one-legged horse, he demanded her name and tried to seize the cow she had with her. However, the woman was the terrible Morrigan, goddess of war, and her anger was the cause of his downfall.

In the world inhabited by mere mortals – humans – the image of a god was believed to actually contain the presence of that god. In this way, to enter a temple was to come near to the god. In ancient Egypt, the image that stood in the innermost shrine was washed, dressed, and offered food each day – a sacred task that only priests or priestesses could perform. Similarly in most cultures, it was through priests that people approached the gods.

Amon, the ancient Egyptian wind god of Thebes, supposedly made a journey each year to his temple at Luxor. His covered image was transported there by his priests. The crowds who watched believed they were seeing the god himself go by.

Shamans and oracles

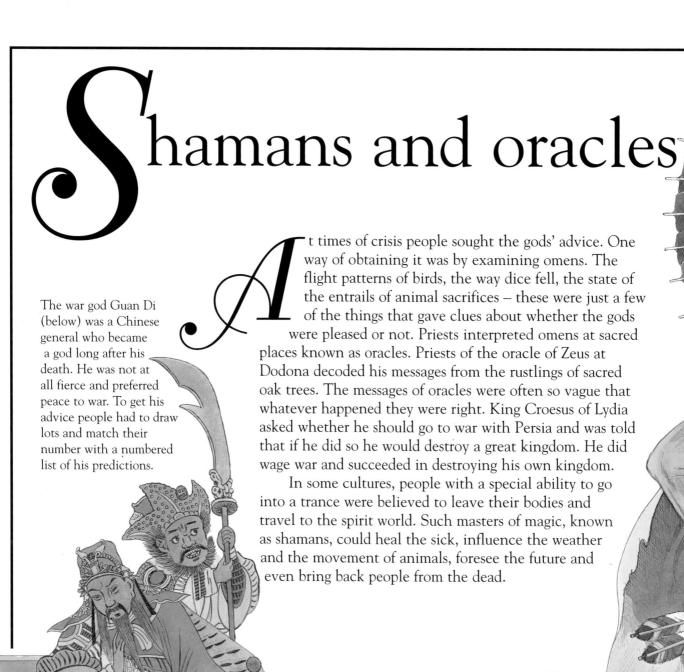

At times of crisis people sought the gods' advice. One way of obtaining it was by examining omens. The flight patterns of birds, the way dice fell, the state of the entrails of animal sacrifices – these were just a few of the things that gave clues about whether the gods were pleased or not. Priests interpreted omens at sacred places known as oracles. Priests of the oracle of Zeus at Dodona decoded his messages from the rustlings of sacred oak trees. The messages of oracles were often so vague that whatever happened they were right. King Croesus of Lydia asked whether he should go to war with Persia and was told that if he did so he would destroy a great kingdom. He did wage war and succeeded in destroying his own kingdom.

In some cultures, people with a special ability to go into a trance were believed to leave their bodies and travel to the spirit world. Such masters of magic, known as shamans, could heal the sick, influence the weather and the movement of animals, foresee the future and even bring back people from the dead.

The war god Guan Di (below) was a Chinese general who became a god long after his death. He was not at all fierce and preferred peace to war. To get his advice people had to draw lots and match their number with a numbered list of his predictions.

A Mayan carving shows a worshipper kneeling before a priest of the plumed serpent god Kukulcan. Rituals like this were believed to bring them into the presence of the god.

The most famous oracle of the ancient world was located in Delphi at the temple of the Greek god Apollo. Questions, written on tablets of lead, were put to the god via a priestess. She seated herself on a tripod, amid fumes that arose from a crack in the ground, and mumbled answers in a trance (right). A priest interpreted – in verse – the meaning of what she said.

Among all native American peoples the 'medicine man' or shaman led rituals which called upon the spirits. With the aid of drums and frenzied dancing, this Plains Indian medicine man (left) would have reached a state of trance that enabled him to enter the spirit world.

An Inuit shaman's charm (above). In times of famine Inuit shamans were said to go to the bottom of the sea and make the sea goddess Sedna release seals to hunt.

Protector spirits
A North American Cheyenne myth

The North American Cheyenne people believe in protector spirits whom they call the 'Listeners Under the Ground'. They say that two of their tribe once met one face to face.

The meeting happened in far distant times, before the Cheyenne had any crops to grow or anything but deer and small creatures to hunt. Life was hard for them and they were often hungry. One day, two hunters out in search of food saw a tall rocky outcrop in the distance and set off to climb it, hoping to catch sight of deer from the top. When they got nearer, they saw that a thundering sheet of water fell from top to bottom in a mighty waterfall.

"Such strong water!" they exclaimed to each other.

"Where can such strength come from?"

The two hunters had never seen such a wonder. The bolder of them decided to find out more. Taking a deep breath he plunged into the wall of water. His companion hesitated, and then dived in after him.

Behind the waterfall they found themselves in another world. On an endless plain of grass an old woman was stirring a pot over a fire. She smiled at them.

"I have been waiting for you," she said, "Your food is ready." She offered them two dishes – one of meat, the other of a yellow porridge. "This is buffalo," she said, "and this is corn."

The taste of the corn was strange but good and the Cheyenne ate hungrily.

"Look to the right" commanded the woman.

They turned and saw a herd of huge beasts grazing on the plain.

"Look to the left" she said, and they saw a field with a tall crop. Then she handed them a bowl of golden seeds.

"Go back to your people," she said. "Give them this corn to plant and tell them I will send them buffalo to hunt. From now on they need not be hungry."

The hunters hurried home, showed the corn and told their story. When the sun rose the next day they saw herds of buffalo streaming over their land, just as the old woman had promised. From that day the Cheyenne were never without food.

Homes of the gods

The gods' earthly homes were their temples, but they also had heavenly dwellings. Even civilisations which worshipped the spirits of natural things believed in some type of greater being or beings who lived far beyond mortal reach. This place was often thought to be in the sky or on a remote and unreachable mountain top. The ancient Greeks believed that Mount Olympus in northern Greece was where their greatest gods lived and that it was the highest mountain in the world. The gods spent their time there feasting and drinking nectar while Apollo, the god of music and poetry, played to them on his lyre. Meanwhile the nine Muses, the lesser goddesses of the arts, sang sweetly to them.

A great deal of feasting also went on in Norse Gladsheim (Joyous Home), the palace that Odin built above the clouds. It stood within Asgard, the Gods' Enclosure, a flowery land in which buildings of solid gold were thatched with silver. Gladsheim was for the male gods while the goddesses had a palace of their own. The gods' land was linked to the earth by a shimmering bridge, Bifrost the Tremulous Way, which humans call a rainbow.

In contrast, Chinese gods lived in a heaven organised very like a government ministry. It was divided into different levels, some say nine, others 33. The most important gods lived on the top level, where the August Personage of Jade held court and granted audiences. Every month, each god had to make a detailed report to his superiors about what he had been doing, and they in turn reported yearly to the August Personage of Jade. He promoted or demoted them as he saw fit. They could even be dismissed.

Temples of the gods

The splendour of the temple of Artemis (below) at Ephesus (in Turkey) made it one of the Seven Wonders of the ancient world. Built in the 4th century BC, it stood on a spot that was sacred to a middle eastern fertility goddess. The Greeks, who settled there from about 1100 BC, accepted her as a form of their hunter-goddess, Artemis.

A temple is both a house for a god or goddess and a place for their worship. People believed that building a temple was a way of ensuring that their god would always be at hand to protect them. For this reason it was important that a temple was the finest building that its designers and builders could achieve. The ancient Egyptians, who made their pharaohs' palaces from mud-brick, built the temples of their gods from stone. The desire to build temples reaching to the sky can be traced throughout history. Five thousand years ago the Sumerians of Mesopotamia were building ziggurats, or temple towers by piling terraces upon terraces, with stairways leading to the temple right at the top. The mound-like stupas of Bhuddist shrines and the many-storied pagodas of Chinese temples were produced with the same goal in mind, while in ancient Greek cities the chief temple was built on the 'acropolis', the highest point.

A majestic gold and ivory statue of Athene stood in her temple (right), the Parthenon, which crowned the Athenian acropolis. Athene was goddess of wisdom and protectress of the city. Athens' ruler Pericles ordered the rebuilding of her temple in 447 BC. He commissioned Phidias, the greatest sculptor of the time, to create the huge statue. The statue has since vanished but the temple remains.

The peoples of Central America built huge stepped pyramids to support the temples of their gods. When the Spaniards arrived in the 16th century they were horrified by evidence of human sacrifices and did their best to destroy the pagan temples. This small one (right) in northern Mexico City is the only Aztec temple that has survived intact.

Gods and goddesses 'facts'

The evil Egyptian god Set was jealous of his brother Osiris who ruled Egypt, and hatched a plot to kill him. He held a feast for the gods, where he produced a magnificent chest which he said was his gift to anyone who could fit inside it. When Osiris got in to try, Set and his supporters clamped down the lid and threw the chest into the sea. Osiris' wife, Isis, wandered the world, found his body and brought it back to Egypt. When Set discovered this he chopped the body into pieces and scattered them throughout the land. However, Isis collected the pieces, put them together and brought her husband to life. Then Ra the sun god made him lord of the underworld.

The Arawak people of the Orinoco river in South America believe that the creator god Kururumany was displeased when he discovered how corrupt and wicked human beings were. He took back his gift of eternal life and sent them diseases and death instead. He also sent snakes and fleas.

Zeus, king of the ancient Greek gods, often argued with his wife Hera, who was jealous of his love affairs. Once she persuaded the other gods on Mount Olympus to plot against him. They bound him with ropes as he lay asleep, and tied them with a hundred knots. While they were planning who should be the next king of the gods, one of them changed their mind and summoned the hundred-handed giant Briareus, who made short work of undoing the knots. Zeus was so furious with his wife that he hung her up from the sky with an anvil fastened to each ankle to weigh her down. He would not free her until the gods made a solemn promise never to rebel again.

Celtic myths tell of the Washer at the Ford. People who met this seemingly harmless figure then knew their death was near. As the Irish hero Cuchulainn rode into battle he saw a young girl washing clothes and armour at a ford. She spoke to him, but seemed not to know him by name, and said that she was washing the armour of Cuchulainn, son of Sualtan, who was to die that day.

The sun goddess Amaterasu was the ancestress of the Japanese imperial family. She overruled the earth god Ohonamoch, son of her brother the Storm god, in order to make her grandson Ninigi the ruler of Japan. He married the goddess of Mount Fugi, and one of their great-grandchildren became Japan's first emperor.

Queen Wang-mu niang niang was the wife of the Chinese god the August Personage of Jade. She presided over the gods' banquets of immortality. There she served the peaches of eternal life that are believed to ripen once every 3,000 years on the peach trees of the imperial orchard.

Hephaestus, the blacksmith god of the ancient Greeks, had a smithy on Mount Olympus. It was from there that Prometheus stole fire to give to mortals. Though Hephaestus was ugly and bad-tempered, he was a superb craftsman. He made a set of golden mechanical women to help him in the smithy. He also made tables with 23 legs which ran by themselves to the meetings of the gods, and ran back again afterwards.

Chinese mythology states that in the beginning there were 10 suns – the 10 children of the god of the eastern sky. They took it in turns to shine each day. One day, feeling bored with their normal routine, all 10 decided to rise together. The earth began to shrivel in their combined heat and the gods, in desperation, summoned Hou I, the Divine

Archer, to shoot them out of the sky. Hou I was so efficient that there would not have been a single sun left if the gods had not sent a swift messenger to stop him. The messenger ran like lightning but was only just in time to snatch the last arrow from Hou I's quiver. This is how one sun was saved to light the world.

The Aborigine people of Australia believe not in one creator but in many – their spirit ancestors who sleep beneath the ground. Long ago, in a period known as the Dreamtime, these spirits rose and travelled about the world, shaping the landscape and creating plants, animals and people.

The heaven described in ancient Chinese beliefs had a god of Salaries and even a god of Examinations. The Examinations god was called K'uei-hsing and he was incredibly ugly. Among his assistants was one known as 'Red Jacket' whose special task was to protect candidates who had not done enough revision.

In the Viking underworld there was an island called Naarstrand, where the terrible ship that would set sail at Ragnarok was being built. The ship was to be made from the toe and finger nails of those who had gone to their death with their nails untrimmed. This meant in order to delay the Day of Doom for as long as possible it was important for people to keep their nails short at all times.

The Yoruba people of western Nigeria believe that in the beginning Orisha the Divine Spirit lived in a house at the foot of a cliff. His servant was Eshu the god of fate. Eshu hated his master and decided to get rid of him. He pushed a boulder over the edge of the cliff so that it fell on the house and crushed Orisha. As Orisha was a god he could not be killed but fragments of him were scattered in all directions. That is why fragments of the divine spirit can be found in all things.

According to the Aztecs the world has seen four ages, or four suns, pass by. The first sun age, the age of the Jaguar, or Earth Sun, was peopled by misshapen giants. The age of the second sun, the Fire Sun, ended with a rain of molten lava. It was followed by the sun age of the Great Winds, which ended in terrible hurricanes. The fourth sun age was the Age of Water. That ended in a flood in which the sky collapsed upon the earth and people turned into fish. The present age, the Age of Earthquakes, will be the last.

43

Glossary

Ainu The native people of northern Japan, who were there before the present Japanese arrived.

Amazonian Belonging to the area around the Amazon River in northern Brazil.

Amulet An ornament or piece of jewellery worn as a charm against evil.

Angola An African country bordering the Atlantic, just south of the equator.

Anvil The iron block on which a blacksmith hammers and shapes his metal.

Apache A native tribe of the southwest of North America.

Aztecs The dominant people of central Mexico in the 16th century.

Brazier A pan or stand holding lighted coals for heating.

Corn In Europe this usually means wheat but in the New World it refers to maize.

Celts The people living in central and western Europe in ancient Greek and Roman times. Except in the far west, their culture was destroyed by the Romans and by invasions from northern Europe.

Cheyenne A native North American people of the Great Plains.

Classical world A term given to the civilisations of the ancient Greeks and Romans.

Entrails The internal parts of an animal.

Hawaii The largest of a group of mid-Pacific islands that form the US state of Hawaii.

Hindu Relating to Hinduism, the religion of many Indians.

Maori The original people of New Zealand, whose ancestors probably came by canoe from the Polynesian islands.

Mayan Belonging to the Maya civilisation of central America. They were at the height of their prosperity from AD 250-950.

Mesopotamia The ancient Greek name for the region which is now known as Iraq. The Sumerian people flourished there from 3100-2000 BC. At various periods from 2000-539 BC the Babylonians or the Assyrians were in power.

Mythology A collection of myths and legends associated with a particular country or culture.

Norse gods The gods of the Teutonic peoples – the ancestors of the Germans, Anglo-Saxons and Scandinavians. Their gods are called 'Norse', because the earliest written accounts of their stories are in Norwegian.

Plains Indians Native American tribes whose homelands (before the Europeans came) were the vast grasslands of central North America.

Polynesia An area made up of widely scattered islands in the central south Pacific Ocean, northeast of New Zealand.

Praying mantis A large insect related to the grasshopper, with long forelegs which fold in a way that suggest it is praying.

Sarcophagus A stone coffin or tomb.

Slovenia The most northern region of former Yugoslavia.

Smithy A blacksmith's workshop, where metal is heated and formed into various objects.

Tahiti An island in the centre of the south Pacific Ocean.

Tripod An ancient Greek three-legged stand supporting a basin or circular surface.

Zaire A large central African country.

Zambia A landlocked country of southern central Africa.

Zapotec A native Central American people whose ancestors created a highly developed civilisation in Mexico from AD 300-900.

Index